WEDDING
Creations

12 PIANO SOLOS TO CELEBRATE LOVE
Arranged by Randall Hartsell

For Ronald Dean Spake

ISBN 978-1-4768-9964-0

WILLIS MUSIC

EXCLUSIVELY DISTRIBUTED BY

HAL•LEONARD®
CORPORATION
7777 W. BLUEMOUND RD. P.O. BOX 13819
MILWAUKEE, WISCONSIN 53213

Visit Hal Leonard Online at
www.halleonard.com

Preface

This collection of wedding music contains my favorite traditional selections as well as three original pieces.

Weddings now take place in a variety of venues; from customary church and religious spaces to hotel ballrooms, from beautiful gardens to exotic island destinations. Often times an organ is not available for use, so the piano or a keyboard provides a logical alternative.

The original integrity of these classical compositions is cherished and admired by everyone, including this composer. These arrangements are not meant to improve on the original compositions, but rather, to help in the performance of these lasting standards by utilizing the range, sonority, and tone quality of the piano. You will hear modern harmonization, creative phrasing, and rhythmic variety. All changes are written to encourage the listener to hear this music in an innovative and fresh way.

While you will surely recognize most of these pieces, the collection begins and ends with an original piece that I hope will also find a place in your wedding repertoire.

My very best wishes,

Randall Hartsell

Contents

Adagio from the Heart

Randall Hartsell

Air
from WATER MUSIC

George Frideric Handel
1685–1759
Adapted and arranged by Randall Hartsell

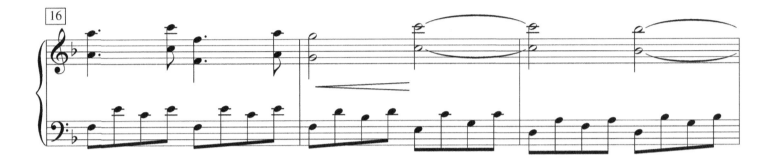

Allegro maestoso
from WATER MUSIC

George Frideric Handel
1685–1759
Arranged by Randall Hartsell

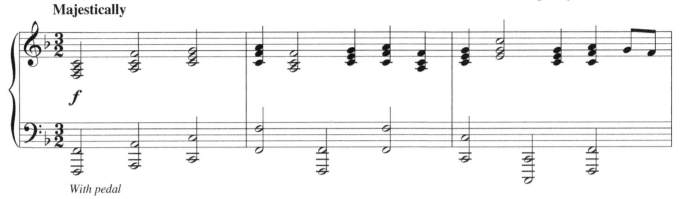

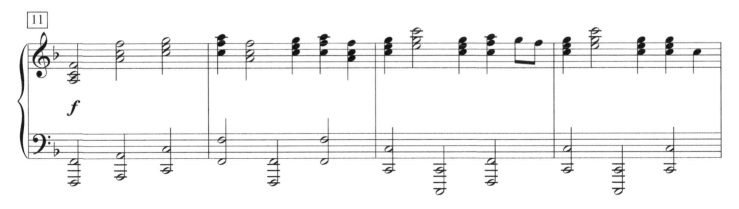

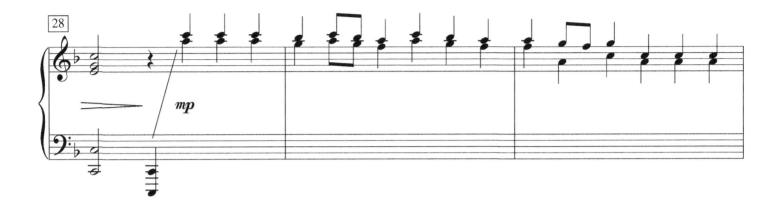

Arioso

Johann Sebastian Bach
1685–1750
Arranged by Randall Hartsell

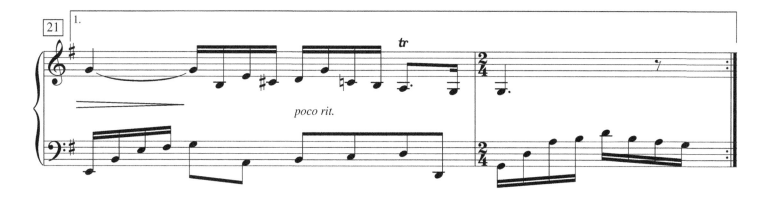

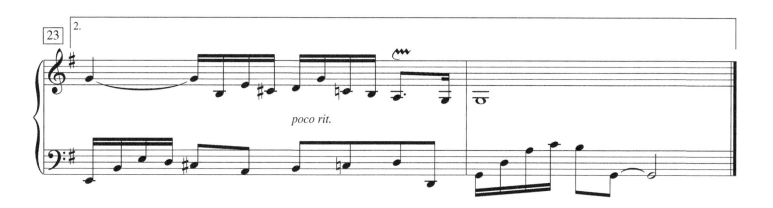

Chanson d'amour

Randall Hartsell

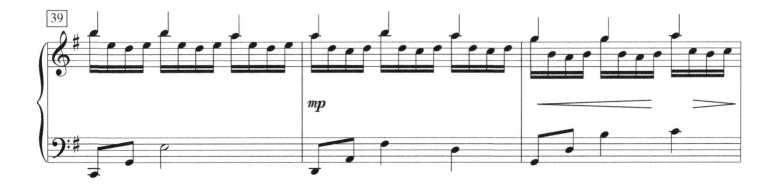

The Heavens Declare

Benedetto Marcello
1686–1739
Arranged by Randall Hartsell

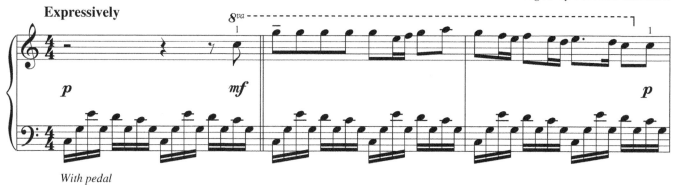

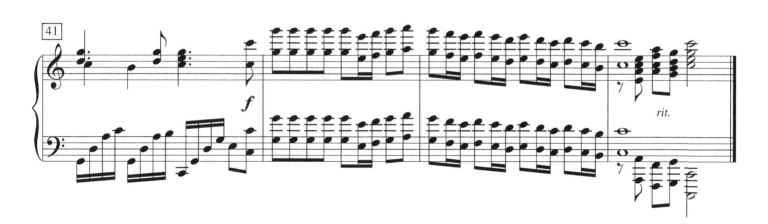

Jesu, Joy of Man's Desiring
from CANTATA NO. 147

Johann Sebastian Bach
1685–1750
Adapted and arranged by Randall Hartsell

Trumpet Voluntary
(The Prince of Denmark's March)

Jeremiah Clarke
1674–1707
Arranged by Randall Hartsell

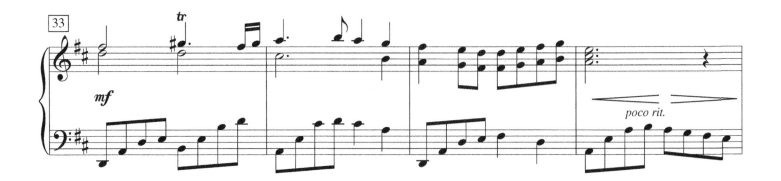

Love Divine, All Loves Excelling

Rowland H. Prichard
1811–1887
Arranged by Randall Hartsell

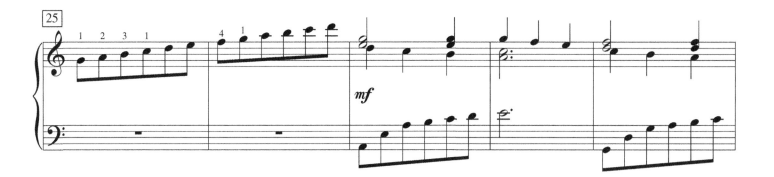

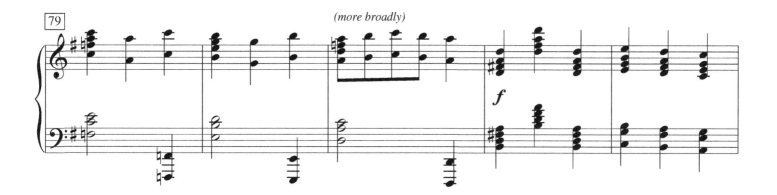

Ode to Joy
from SYMPHONY NO. 9

Ludwig van Beethoven
1770–1827
Arranged by Randall Hartsell

Moderately, with exuberance

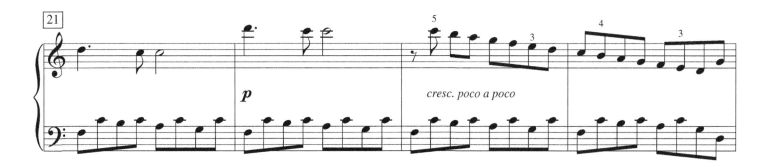

36

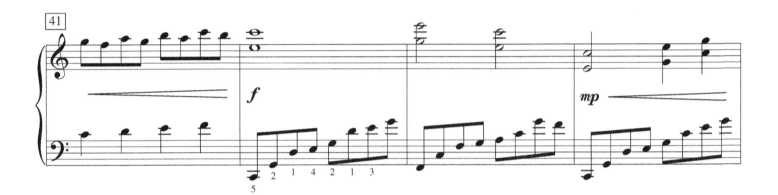

Rondeau

Jean-Joseph Mouret
1682–1738
Arranged by Randall Hartsell

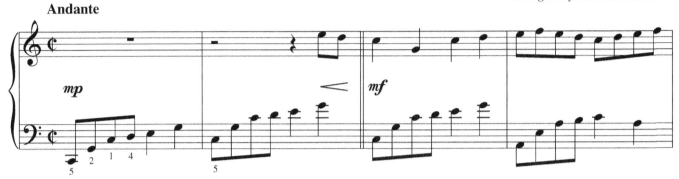

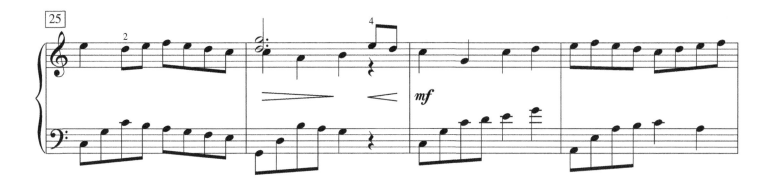

Unity of Love

Randall Hartsell

Moderately, with warmth

p espressivo

mp

With pedal

mf

poco rit.

mp a tempo

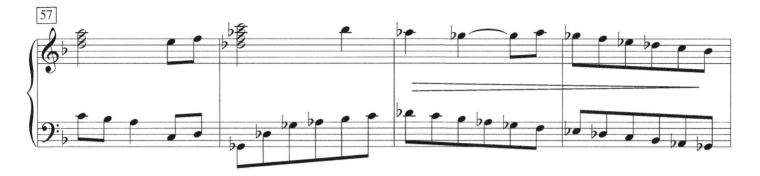

CLASSIC PIANO REPERTOIRE

The *Classic Piano Repertoire* series includes popular as well as lesser-known pieces from a select group of composers out of the Willis piano archives. Every piece has been newly engraved and edited with the aim to preserve each composer's original intent and musical purpose.

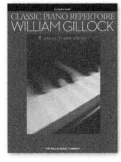

WILLIAM GILLOCK - ELEMENTARY
8 Great Piano Solos
Dance in Ancient Style • Little Flower Girl of Paris • On a Paris Boulevard • Rocking Chair Blues • Sliding in the Snow • Spooky Footsteps • A Stately Sarabande • Stormy Weather.
00416957 ....$8.99

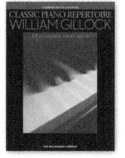

WILLIAM GILLOCK - INTERMEDIATE TO ADVANCED
12 Exquisite Piano Solos
Classic Carnival • Etude in A Major (The Coral Sea) • Etude in E Minor • Etude in G Major (Toboggan Ride) • Festive Piece • A Memory of Vienna • Nocturne • Polynesian Nocturne • Sonatina in Classic Style • Sonatine • Sunset • Valse Etude.
00416912 .... $12.99

EDNA MAE BURNAM - ELEMENTARY
8 Great Piano Solos
The Clock That Stopped • The Friendly Spider • A Haunted House • New Shoes • The Ride of Paul Revere • The Singing Cello • The Singing Mermaid • Two Birds in a Tree.
00110228 ....$8.99

EDNA MAE BURNAM - INTERMEDIATE TO ADVANCED
13 Memorable Piano Solos
Butterfly Time • Echoes of Gypsies • Hawaiian Leis • Jubilee! • Longing for Scotland • Lovely Senorita • The Mighty Amazon River • Rumbling Rumba • The Singing Fountain • Song of the Prairie • Storm in the Night • Tempo Tarantelle • The White Cliffs of Dover.
00110229 .... $12.99

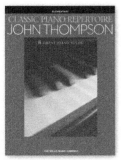

JOHN THOMPSON - ELEMENTARY
9 Great Piano Solos
Captain Kidd • Drowsy Moon • Dutch Dance • Forest Dawn • Humoresque • Southern Shuffle • Tiptoe • Toy Ships • Up in the Air.
00111968 ....$8.99

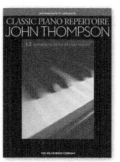

JOHN THOMPSON - INTERMEDIATE TO ADVANCED
12 Masterful Piano Solos
Andantino (from Concerto in D Minor) • The Coquette • The Faun • The Juggler • Lagoon • Lofty Peaks • Nocturne • Rhapsody Hongroise • Scherzando in G Major • Tango Carioca • Valse Burlesque • Valse Chromatique.
00111969 .... $12.99

LYNN FREEMAN OLSON - EARLY TO LATER ELEMENTARY
14 Great Piano Solos
Caravan • Carillon • Come Out! Come Out! (Wherever You Are) • Halloween Dance • Johnny, Get Your Hair Cut! • Jumping the Hurdles • Monkey on a Stick • Peter the Pumpkin Eater • Pony Running Free • Silent Shadows • The Sunshine Song • Tall Pagoda • Tubas and Trumpets • Winter's Chocolatier.
00294722 ....$9.99

LYNN FREEMAN OLSON - EARLY TO MID-INTERMEDIATE
13 Distinctive Piano Solos
Band Wagon • Brazilian Holiday • Cloud Paintings • Fanfare • The Flying Ship • Heroic Event • In 1492 • Italian Street Singer • Mexican Serenade • Pageant Dance • Rather Blue • Theme and Variations • Whirlwind.
00294720 ....$9.99

WILLIS MUSIC

EXCLUSIVELY DISTRIBUTED BY

HAL•LEONARD®

CLOSER LOOK
View sample pages and hear audio excerpts online at www.halleonard.com

www.willispianomusic.com

www.facebook.com/willispianomusic

Prices, content, and availability subject to change without notice.

Biography

RANDALL HARTSELL is a graduate of East Carolina University
where he studied piano pedagogy and performance. His publications
are influenced by many years of teaching experience, and the
sweeping lyrical lines and sound technical structures in his music
appeal often to both student and teacher.

Mr. Hartsell has taught piano at Pfeiffer University in Misenheimer,
North Carolina, and has accompanied numerous dance classes and
performances at UNC Charlotte. Currently, he operates a private
studio in the Charlotte area, is a clinician for Willis Music, and
serves as an officer for the Charlotte Piano Teachers Forum.